# ALISON FELL

## Kisses for Mayakovsky

Published by VIRAGO PRESS Limited 1984
41 William IV Street, London WC2N 4DB

Copyright © Alison Fell 1984

All rights reserved

**British Library in Cataloguing Data**
Fell, Alison
    Kisses for Mayakovsky.
    I. Title
    821'.914        PR6056.E4/

    ISBN 0-86068-593-4

Printed in Great Britain by
The Anchor Press, Tiptree, Essex
Typeset by Rowland Phototypesetting Limited
Bury St Edmunds, Suffolk

Some of the poems in this collection have appeared in *Smile Smile Smile Smile, Licking the Bed Clean, Bread and Roses, One Foot on the Mountain, Cutlasses and Earrings, Writing Women, City Limits, Pluto Disarmament Diary, Refractory Girl, Autonomie, Change Internationale.*

# Contents

## Burning questions

You are a lynx and a liar
and I have my father's dancing eyes
and laughter crackles between us
like snakes or lightning
in the quick dab of lip

Laughing we touch and fly:
we are buzzing and crafty,
uncatchable.

Laughing we deny
what is darkest in us,
the word's strong shadow,
the need to choose.

What shall we do with each other?

I know the shock of the future
and the whistling silence.
I do not know you.
You may be translucent,
I may pass right through.

Sit down and settle,
Let me melt into you.
You must tell me your truths
and see if I sting.

## The wish

In my dream
I travelled east
to the far end of Russia;
I watched flat trucks of lumber pass,
and the chained logs creaked
and the thrashed leaves flew up
like a message

I saw a wooden jetty
there, waterlogged on
that Manchurian rim,
jutting over the silted stones
and the crabs. Out to sea,
no sails or trade,
only a memory of
whalers and my father

And on the shelf of the shore,
slanting like a long wish,
a mailbox stood askew
in the warp of weathers:
a tarpaulin lid banging loose
a blue letter
a promise of return

# Desire

The wind is strong enough to move wasps.
This blowing branch is mine,
silvery thing, all mine,
my teethmarks swarm over it:
what sweet sap and small beetles racing.

Mother warns me I will get worms
from this zest
for chewing and digesting
fur buds and the satin
leaves of beech, from all this
testing and possessing.
'Stop that,' she says,
'Stop this minute. See the
wee eggs you'll swallow!'

My needle-bright eye is rash
and scans greedily,
sees pine-cones lose pollen
in yellow gusts;
the loch's rim has a
curd of it, the face of
the middle deeps is
skimmed with dust and wrinkles.

The birch trunk wears a
sleeve of paper, clear-layered,
like sunburned skin – a wrap.
It streams from my thumbnail
till the wind snatches it.

# *Girl's gifts*

The soft whorls of my fingertips
against snapdragons:
I am making a flower basket for my grandmother.
A rose petal folds back, squares, curls under
One, two, many rose petals curl back
between my fingers
I search for the core which hides.
My grandmother is gentle today,
old. Bees hum over her.
Today she sits reading, not gardening,
not scolding.
The blossom on its branch holds juice which
a touch spills
I glance across the grass,
a shadow in the window is my mother
cooking, watching.
I am making a tiny secret basket for my grandmother.
My mouth waters
I would lick the green leaf, taste the bronze
and yellow silk of my snapdragon,
I mould petals, weave stems, with love
my little finger inches in the folds:
it is done, red and gold.
I will carry it cupped like a jewel or a robin's egg
It will lie, perfect, in her wrinkled palm
I will cross the grass and give it.

## *Suspicion*

This terrible alertness
sours the milk in me,
binds lips, tears
a barb across the heart.
What is to be trusted
if mothering breeds
hatred at the core?
This pap and pretence
is bitter food.

What is to be hoped for
when the lovely twist
of hawthorns
warns
only of trickery,
and bark peels
to a pith of spite?

My grim eye strips
the gifts women bring
and in the bread and smiles
sees hidden worms lie.

## Our luck

There you are!
sourpuss morning face
displacing
three days of signs
in this poltergeist April
when magpies fight the
blundering wind
and trees throw branches
thick as thighs
to powder on the road ahead

All weekend
like marbled warm hens
how cosy we've been
in our borrowed car –
such privilege

I want you to say it is our luck

I'll teach you to bow
to the new moon
cross fingers against surprises
and the evil eye

You can laugh at my jitters
I don't mind

I'll give you the rain
trees       wood anemones
three times a day
like medicine

## *two women think back*

the woman on the TV screen
deliberates     her bedroom
wall blue as midnight
dotted symmetrically
with white stars

she touches her face
her hair     she remembers
her marriage
exactly
how he peeled her stocking
down
over her ankle

she weeps

the woman in the armchair
watches     moored
to her short moon shadow
she touches     her arm
the excellence of her belly

yes it was sweet
that one

she wishes that any marriage
might be remembered so

exactly

by its inconvenient
hurlings     the willing
legs white idiots
in the air     the sweet
black scratch of love and lace

# Rannoch Moor

Behind us, Glencoe of the Slaughter,
Achnacone, field of dogs,
Achtriachan, where the water-bull
lurks among thin fish tickled by weed,
and the Great Herdsman of Etive
over us like a black axe

To pace the moor, and mark it,
like a cat bruises the grass
for its bed,
or be claimed instead –
scars of burnt heather, dead
weariness, the sheep paths
misleading, and the bogs pitted
with white water

Slow steps mark the line
on the moor sour with struggle,
where darkness is brought to the brim,
and the bog cotton bursts
like puffs of smoke after a
musket,
and the broken bleached roots
of the old forest
are white bones under
the petrol shimmer of methane

*The Great Herdsman of Etive – Buchaille Etive Mor – is a mountain at the east
end of Glencoe*

Slow march in the whine
of telegraph wires,
while the wind chops at my breath
and the peat mud sticks to my feet
like rafts


## *Saturday Night Fever*

Tonight I am all and always
dancer, a streak of a girl
shearing stars,
I'll kick a few out of
orbit
now I can make my real clatter
Mercury's grand to jive with,
and tap-dancing,
there's a thing!
– watch my bright rocket-feet.
I'll slew like fountains,
a feast of fireworks
each joint cradles quicksilver
each bone a hot song

Tomorrow limps
there's a stone in my shoe
no, a rock, jesus, a slagheap
Years of lead
Years of dread

## Figure in Space, by Giacometti

The art student
in bed with her anatomy books
eats white bread and sugar sandwiches.
She pecks white sugar grains
from the pages of bones
and pale plaster scabs
from the moons of her nails

She has forgotten how to speak

She keeps a slush of grey clay
in the kitchen sink
and a postcard pinned
to the wall –
Figure in Space,
with a stride like
open scissors

She will die for Art, starve
for it, they warned her
it might be necessary

They did not say also
that Giacometti was a big man,
muscled, ate like a bear,
enjoyed his lovely wife

On the main street people
loom like hams,
jellied and pink

She will not go out

She will work by the wall
with her stride like scissors
figure
less figure
armature of bird bones
space
more space

## Farther, higher, louder

I woke from a dream
in which someone said my name
and there was May rain
at the front window,
hail at the back.
Farther, sang the voice against glass,
higher, and louder,
twisting me small
in a ball
under a low settee

Lodged like a hedgehog
I read books backwards
and think of Nijinsky –
he fell like a bat,
bruised and blinded

In the ache of the seasons'
unstable bonding
I sit prickling
pins and needles
the circulation fighting for life
the dead legs begging to be remembered
and to move

## Stripping blackcurrants

On a garden rug tinged with amber
your bare skin
grows a red fur.
Half a lilac leaf
sticks to your belly.

Stripping blackcurrants, the berries
split
and stain my fingers
as the stalks
tear from the fruit.

I have a yellow mane which crackles
and brown breasts
freckled as eggs.

Pushing among the leaves, I imagine
their feather fingers
as deft as yours.

Your body haunts the corner
of my eye:
books, papers, your bent head.
I want you in heat,
sticky as blackcurrants.

Deep in the tang of the bush
I remember the taste of your ear.
How you angled your neck
to offer it.

I flaunt my golden back.
It glows from within, a raging aura.
Unbelievable, how you resist me.

You read.
The bush catches fire.

## And again

The man with the big mouth
and the ribbon-elastic legs
has bowled me over

His tongue running in my mouth
is sweet as a bean

The bare branch of his forearm
sets me sweating
My pores open: no shelter

He's a dark man,
melancholic and bitter;
with a hornet's sting
he bites to the bone

Dreadful in suspicion,
he becomes a leech
– he will have me,
he sings it to the telephone wires

Since last year I've grown
cautious
and knowledgeable:
ruefully I refuse him

The child stamps and wails out,
mourning the trust of his fragrance –
the true skin,
indisputable
as jasmine in the dark

# Directive

In the great night
of the city
a black girl with
a frizz fringe
snow-loaded
walks raggedly
under the whalebone arch
of street lamps

'A flat image projected on the retina'

As spiral scribbles of
colour and atom
we flutter and settle
gathering wits and weight
into the world of
bracelet
collar on the dog
the elastic belt whittling the waist
the tears crumpled into the centre of the tissue

the lips surround the cigarette
the crowds surround the Pope

There are brides in the back
of black taxis
their gloved hands like
white mice
in the blur of their laps

'give us bread, but give us roses'

Hurry to make the moment simple
brass tacks

    'the Allied armies advanced remorselessly on the Rhine'

Down
goes the hawk to its prey
the ball
the apple from the tree
the sailor to the bottom of the sea

Impatience my vice
my head full of smoke
rattlings
rule of the gun, greed, tank treads

    the fingers close round the
    nipple
    trigger

# For my sister, who emigrated

The rags
of our chiffons
tearing between us,
the pearls of our games
unstrung

(Do you remember how
in the night the tart
from the saloon
dressed in leather
to lead raids?)

The hazardous yards
of three oceans
yawning between us:
round world into which
you raced early, eager
to trace the difficult
geography of men and women,
hard games of the older girls.

I have wiped the slate clean,
written books from which
you were omitted

But now your voice on the phone:
high twang of the cattle ranch

(Do you remember how
in the night the farmer
rode his black and secret stallion
and the sheriff turned outlaw?)

Over these three seas,
over thirteen years
there floats between us

a shoebox of cardboard
with a cargo of
bandits, cowgirls,
and plasticine corrals,
and cabins woven of reeds
where paper ladies go to
change their cut-out gowns

## For myself

In her
thirty-three year old
long grown
prime,
still the gnarled
changeling
peeks from her
cot,
ugly as a turnip
sheep-gnawed,
little sprout
which grew
in the dark
lives hardy through
frost,
etched
with a breadknife,
lonely as
black Hallowe'en,
fire hungers
in her lantern
eyes

# The victors (October 18, 1977)

What greater glory
than this
morning over
Bonn
with the sun
all in order
on the ranked
walnut trees
over
Mogadishu
and the three
slight shadows
on the airstrip
Dead
three more rebels
blood and sand
in their gullets
Dumb
three more silences
for the State

What greater glory
than this
morning over
Stammheim
with the sun
ekeing down
through gutters
slits
bars
blockhouses.

The chalkdust
hangs in sunbeams
marks time
marks place
marks corpses
gone
three more rebels
Baader          shot
Ensslin         hanged
Raspe           shot
And Schmidt
by the ugly glint
of black cars
smiles to the
whirl of newsreel
how he rode
the night and won;
by drinking Coca-Cola
smoking sigaretten
taking snuff
made in Austria
by British mixers.
Callaghan simpers,
twinkles back victory,
'A wonderful morning
for us all'

Six more silences
for the State,
the wrong voices
stilled
and the grey-faced liars
whirr out murder
till the roar
of right
deafens
us.

# The bad omen

When the knife came
with your sheepish note
reminding me of the one
you lost in the dust of France
I knew that it was over.

I am familiar with the guilt
of men, the bluster
with the blade at the heart,
the dodging apology.
In dreams my muffled
fist flails: you put me
in the wrong, you cotton-wool
boy, every mother's son
with your white irreproachable smile
slaking the older ladies

I remember those lapses, when
the air took and shook you
dry like rattlepods:
loss of keys and charms,
the sudden shrieking attacks
on mosquitos and my tenderest fusses

I remember the sway of the train,
blue blue overalls of fishermen;
the punishing rain on the tent roof
as I thrust myself into your mouth.
Why did I entrust myself to you?
You who didn't even know
never to send a knife to a friend.

## Pomegranate time

Pomegranate time     cold fruit
short grace before winter

In the market
the greengrocer's hands are
stained red with beetroot

Sun through smoke of asphalt
the leaves float and dazzle

Already the days are a thin
sliver rescued from night,
the air is narrower,
piercing

The child sneezing in its pushchair
has seen a golden riddle

Twisting in its harness
twisting in its new layers
it stares

at the wheels where the
wet leaves stick,
shining and turning

## Sail away

Sail away, tough mama,
you never were the starlight
mama of my dreams.

How short your legs are:
on the street your little feet
trot: clip clop. How irritating
to slow my pace for you.
I go in bounds.

But you were the one who slipped away
joking, through the check-in,
and soon you'll span the sky.
It's all topsy-turvy,
there are holes just everywhere.

We never suited each other
and we don't fit yet.
I rattle at the stones you
won't look under;
you see a queer stick,
odd daughter,
a questioning thing.

The experiment's over
The wings tear the plane
from the ground.
We must be steel now, for our
separate adventures –
a right pair of steam-hammers,
and the pact lies in that.

So hold steady, tough mama,
sail away,
You never were the starlight mama of my dreams.

# Proof positive

5 kilometres north of Angoulême
on the Route Nationale Dix
a blizzard of moths
occludes the windscreen

Either it is snowing or it is not snowing.
A logical proposition.
Either I am a white storm around you
or I am not.
(Proof?)

The baby in my lap asks simpler questions:
where the sky has gone,
and why the stars are flying.

The moths flow away
on the slipstream.
The shift of the moon,
red to yellow.

The drawn gaze,
the illusion of movement suspends decisions.

I see you like moon or moth,
coloured by longing.
Either we are floating or we are not
floating
towards the dawn.

# *Significant fevers*

A January night. Moonlight
strikes the window. Six sweaters
heaped on the chair,
two pairs of jeans each
containing crumpled knickers.

*Proper* little girls don't lose their clothes,
the text in the head goes; they fold them
the night before, they dream of piles
of linen neat as new exercise books.

Hot-head, scaly-skinned,
feeble and feverish,
I toss under the weight of quilts.

Liz rings up miserable,
comes round with lemons and whisky.
Her blouse has an ironed crease
down the outside of each sleeve.

Lévi-Strauss if I understand him right
says that women disrupt the man-made
opposition between nature and culture.

We nod and drink whisky. The
significance of the fever mounts.

There's no word for the feeling women
have of being in the wrong before
they even open their mouths,
Dale Spender says.

Provisional love. Too much of nothing
can make a woman ill-at-ease.
I'm feeling – *warren,*
*hollowburnt.* I object to this
set-up, let it be said.

The pale princess on her timid
bed never talks back.
She's dying, but
terribly pleased you asked.

Life is short as a shoelace,
but who knows it?
'68' I say, 'the politics of desire –
will we see it again?'
Liz says she wants everything *now,*
everything on offer.
Both of us agree that what we
would most relish at the moment
is to be madly desired. We feel
in the wrong about this too.

Lonelyhearts, Classified:
John, 34, interests publishing, astrology,
walking. Own car, limited income.
Seeks intelligent feminist 20-40,
Box Y288.

I disagree with Liz: No,
they can't all be creeps.
I'm feeling – *oldmould, grabbitted.*

In the West, much was made
of killing dragons. St George
and the other heroes with all
their hardware, littering
the ley lines with sites
of slaughter and canonisation.

In the structures of fever,
never a dull moment.
(The spiral round the stone,
the spiral deep in the storm)

In the East they bound
women's feet and believed
in the harmony of man and landscape,
paths of wind, water and dragons,
forces which must not be impeded
by rails, tramways, television aerials.

Sweat stains the sheets. I
have boils, Liz has cold sores:
energies seeking escape routes.

Clean neckties of news announcers,
rescuing us from dragons.
Clean underpants. A consensus.
Under the newsdesk their toes
manipulate electric trainsets.

*Proper* little girls don't lose their clothes,
the text in the dream goes.
I'm feeling – *ragbitter,*
*hellworthy.*

The nuclear train which is found
on no timetable sidles
through London in the night,
containing dead hearts blazing:
an energy which has been eaten
and will eat.

Watching the commercials, we note
the speed of the assault, messages
addressed to envy and ego.
We toast each other, high-heeled monsters,
and no country we can name.

'What is good and bad taste is very subjective,'
an ITV executive explains,
of ads shown during a play about women in Auschwitz.
'Of course we ruled out several categories
immediately – no food or vitamins,
hair preparations, holiday camps,
or gas products of any kind.'
His smile oils the screen.

Clawing at the pillows and the heaped
quilts, *High time*, I say, that the
dragon took hands with the pale princess –
shadow victim defended (sometimes) by
men and lances and smiling
back, always smiling –
*first strike* in a
quest selfish and long
negative to positive
(I never knew her name)

Take       eat       speak       act

(The spiral deep in the storm,
the world turning over)

# Yorkshire Dales, Easter

*(for Marsha)*

We walked in moonland
while the grouse raged at us
black peat sprung our heels
white silt of limestone seeped

and everywhere a rumble of change:
landslips, frogs' spawn,
ooze of sap.

Walking side by side was easy,
with no shocks
the land could not absorb.

Diverting you,
I poked at lichens
at tree-clefts
that rot or ants had chewed.

But then the shyest hand in the world
reached over.
I sought it, I feared it –
careful kiss of friendship,
woman to woman. This time,
you were close in.

I thrust will against the flinch,
breathed air,
leaned into this extraordinary
faltering bond.
(Grumble of change, whispers
in the bracken
where no wind shook it.)

I was dizzy, trying to laugh or swallow,
on these elephant rocks,
on that scarp where the sky
wheeled over.


## *deer forest*

the blue pines shiver
under fighter planes
the cornfields are cut to white
the rosehips a red arch above me

be quiet
I am listening
for the scratch of antlers

how many trees crushed
to make those letters
you choke me with?
paper flags stabbing at me
paper aeroplanes

be quiet
I am waiting
in the still place under the bridge
I am waiting
for the sky to rush

I am the star you desire in hatred
to name
to stamp
to claim
I am the flint underfoot to savage
your mad goat's heels

# Border raids

*(for my grandmother)*

Fierce pins plough her hair
You can tell by the angry drag
of the net
that once she was beautiful,
envied and glad of it
The nightingale of the county,
electrifying the village halls

She told me she wore winged hats
tall as gladioli,
and the hanging moon sang with her,
and how they clapped and horded
at her doors

When she went,
she went like the old bunch, cursing,
blue as smoke,
you could almost smell the burning
(Oh, they were a wild lot, the Johnstones,
border raiders,
horse stealers setting the Kirk alight
and all their enemies inside)

With her heart tattered
as a tyre on the road
she begged for morphine
and to be done with it,
to be gone among the gliding dead

She glints now in the gooseberry bushes,
her broom hisses out at low-dashing cats
In the night she slaps up her window
and hurls hairbrushes

I've been thinking
If I could go back,
stealing up the cemetery hill
to borrow back her bones,
I'd give her to the merry gods
of the midsummer garden
who dance among the columbines
who fib and fart
and I'd tell them to trumpet her out

## Supper

There is the curdling sky
and the green spry beans
finger-long and knuckled
and the bird's flat fleeting path
across my window
and still
you will not come

# *The cliff*

The speedwell is blue
in the new bracken,
where midsummer's loose
tumble of daisies
tangles the incline

How good to know
how to shift under the wind,
to be shaken
and rooted

The gull's steep wing
climbs unseen currents,
over the haygatherers
on the headland
and the cattle strayed
in the curling thorn

Three times he will hover
over the prickled cushions
of gorse
and the pink shiver of thrift

Three times he will dive
with his black eye
beating the land flat
and slowing the sea
to a snail's pace

and then he will point south
and slide fast
over the slanting thickets

How good to know
when to go
at the gull's pace

or grow slow-spiralling
as the hawthorn

to enter the deep and
stinging violet
of the nettle's stem
or drift empty
into the salt air

## *Surface tension*

1.  Since she was warned of the danger
    her belly holds desire like a
    bomb in the back seat of a car.
    Her skin too thin for collisions
    is a diaphragm dividing chemicals.

2.  Ten days of the month she is
    lustier than any hero, yeasty,
    all cunt. Her glycerine hips
    hint and swagger. She's a huntress;
    a knife grins in her teeth
    but her hands are tied.

3.  On the surface they stalk tall,
    the tension webbing them.
    She turns tail, diving for
    avenues of grass, to nose
    among slugs for the wet secrets
    of dawn and mushrooms.
    Or seeking air, she leaps too high
    and skims in the chinks
    of the gates of day
    in her new blue iridescent madness.

# Friend

In the white morning
we cuddle in our warm
world, toes friendly
in a hoard of blankets,
thighs glossing each other,
bums amiable. Me, I am starved
as a sparrow
after the long cold,
while the snow drives at
tree-trunks,
whirls at my window-sashes,
so fine
it spins
in the cracks and corners
of my house.

Up here
we are in a high galleon
on the crust
of a vanished country.
The sky is iron
behind birds, the road
a track of ash, cracking with
salt, and a scrape and
bang of spades echoes against
the black blocks of streets.


This light
bleaches and blues
skin; our noses of frost
collide.

You are no bully
to dig and spoil, but still
I warn you, some paths
are closed, impassable.

Between my house and yours
lies a city of snowfields;
still I need your steady
heat to set against
the bitterness of winter.

# *The weight*

Whole days gone while
the world goes on and I
go under;
carpets have interstices,
floors are quicksands,
bottomless

down, down, the lead baby
goes dangling,
to plumb caverns where
the woman-mountain waits.
Still stone she draws
me down

– let me go, let me grow older

as rocks we rub, hopeless,
scarring each other.
It is a mothering cold as death
and incoherent,
here, without air or sun or sap.
She will wear me round her neck
for years yet,
ugly ornament which clanks
and chafes

– let me go, let me lighten,
let my breasts drift up
like dry leaves

## Old dreadful

I can't stop it.
The night drags down on
me and
the beast is out;
scraggy, cawing
for man-flesh or
someone-skin.
What an endeavour,
living with this nag under
the rafters.
(Normally it nests quietly
enough, sullen
in the straw and shade,
I feed it chocolate
slyly.)
Now it booms round the
room and plops down,
romps sideways, an old flirt
in thin feathers,
tucks its head under the
arms of strangers, points
a claw, wheedling,
nudges, thrusts up
its red mouth wide.

# *Atlanta streets*

The timidest man owns streets
with his eyes – headlights sweeping
breasts, lips, thighs –
they dip only for a bigger bruiser.

Our lowered eyelids hide murder.

Outside a drugstore in Atlanta
one thug tried it on, for him
we waited, four of us fringing
the sidewalk, gangsters in the
shadows. One flung a chocolate malted
in his face, he lunged
kicked her down while we paused
(everyone hesitates who fears the murder
in her) but only for the time the bright
sour pink of a police car beacon
takes to spin once,
and then these sisters beat and clawed him
down and when he tried to run
I caught his coat-tails
and he spun back, roaring,
in an arc
into their fists again
and still I stalled there –
until his buddy came to even up
the odds, then I was ready, but then
there was glass shattering
and the ruby razor neck of a
Coke bottle crooked up, glistening
and obscene,

and wise blacks hanging back
and white folks coming close – to
gawp? defend? who? us? him?
the staggering ravaged guy?
And now it was time to run, vault,
dodge trash, make
scant wind in the
still city dark, to the
car-park, rev through the underpass
shudder out to the
Freeway's tungsten howl


## knife

---

knife my warm handle knife my clasp tight knife my
stroke easy knife my warm cheek my cool blade knife
my flat of the hand knife my slap my safe knife my
finger and thumb no slice i am trim knife my good eye
knife my fly straight knife i am i am my good eye daddy
girl knife my don't cry my see it fly knife my throw my
show it off knife do you like i am my slice my rasp
knife my pink i am i am my dare my red will come knife
my daddy eye good girl knife see it i am i am my blood
my brave my rasp see it my pink pith knife dare do you
like me do you like my gash

# In confidence

*(for the Writers' Group)*

– An orgasm is like an anchovy,
she says,
little, long, and very salty.

– No, it's a caterpillar,
undulating, fat and sweet.

– A sunburst, says the third,
an exploding watermelon:
I had one at Christmas.

– Your body betrays, she says,
one way or another.
Rash and wriggling, it comes
and comes, while your mind
says lie low, or go.

– Or else it snarls and shrinks
to the corner of its cage
while your mind, consenting,
whips it on and out,
out in the open
and *so* free.

– As for me,
says the last,
if I have them brazen
with birthday candles,
with water faucets
or the handles of Toby Jugs,
I don't care who knows it.
But how few I have –
keep *that* in the dark.

# TGV, Paris–Avignon

See, we are orange as angels,
crazy-coloured and high
over the spinning spires
Below us the daisies streak
by, comet-tailed, our sound
is thin and long as a gasp
We are fingernails on glass
The glow in the crack
of the door, the tug
of trains. We are the tease
and hurt of the moon
We are mad malice
and we shine

*For Maria Burke (who knocked at the door while I was writing about the alienation of life in the cities under capitalism)*

---

Maria, in search of hospitality:
I opened the door a crack
she stood there in the dark
dribbling a bit.
'We're in need of somewhere to stay.'
She was alone. It was winter.
She wore plimsolls, her bare legs
were hairless.
'I used to know some man who lived here.
It's a squat, isn't it.'
'No, not a squat,' I snapped,
'And who was the man?'

The powerful deeply suspect
the powerless
of manipulations and lying.

'You should come in from the cold.'
Maria's eyes were fixed,
glassy on largactyl.
I phoned some hostels;
she knew them all and
loathed them, said she'd crouch
by frozen trees in the park
rather than go there.
'I went to a house I used to
live in, it was all pulled down.'

Clocks and towers loom over her
Homes shudder and tumble around her.

Her hands shook eating soup.
She accepted tea.
'It's the drug makes me shake.'
She'd hitched from a mental home
in Manchester, heading for another
in Southall, which didn't want her.
'I've a letter from the consultant.
Will you phone for me, tell him
I'm coming in?'
It was dated last June,
it said merely, 'Dear Maria,
it was pleasant to see you
at the hospital today. What
I explained to you is that the drug
is a chemical which acts
on the brain and is necessary
to stabilise the thought processes.'

'It's my only home,' said
the orphan angrily, 'I know
they don't want me
but I'm going in. I was there . . .
I lived there . . . three years.'
I showed her the spare room
she thanked me several times
stripped to her bra while
I was still there.
Only those with homes are entitled
to modesty, the consultant
is modest, his wife is modest
her body belongs to him only;
Maria's belongs to anyone:
the mouth to nurses who feed it
the head to doctors who shock it
the nipple to drivers on the open road
who pluck it
the smooth skin to the casual helper.

The consultant, who has all he needs,
considers her promiscuous, recoils
from the glare of her love that
stares from her eyes, seeking.
He reaches for a prescription pad;
this winter, he decides,
Maria must stand on
her own two plimsolls.

Maria gathering up
selves scattered like
grit on the roadside
doodles darkness
and a cottage with lit windows,
gropes and pines for her
three-minute-a-fortnight
father.

## *visit from the antipodes*

is it simply because you're coming
that night after night
I dream of being claimed?

as if a switch had been thrown
the pictures flicker back:
the 'fifties marcasite on your black dress
suspender bumps

and I the wolf-child
prowling on packed snow
shimmying stones over the midnight ice

and the snowmen, for delight –
white suitors in the morning yard
with cinder eyes to spin you
round, as debonair as anything

my igloo, too, my hands
never idle, my clever tracery
of sticks and making
on that long ravenous wait to win you

in my factory for happiness
I am mixing you rich as a pudding
I am dressing you like a Christmas tree
you will stretch out your arms and shine

# 'Il y a longtemps qu'on fait de la politique'

Humming a French song – French-Canadian
that is – remember? I seek out the fireworks.
'Est-ce que vous savez, madame,
où sont les feux d'artifice?'
– Telling you how I love to be
swept along gay and helpless
behind the baggy-trousered brass band
and the majorettes' fluorescent batons,
how torches and fireflies disarm me.

'It could be Babi Yar,' you growl,
dragging your feet through the fairground,
and the spangled night swings about,
and all innocents are criminals

Il y a longtemps qu'on fait de la politique –
Granted;
but need you remind me always
of the dangers of enchantment?
Can't we take holidays occasionally?
Aren't we safe enough here in France
where there's a *kind* of socialism
and uniforms never ever fit
and the majorettes are out of step
and the small boy trombonist
ties up his shoelace in the middle of the encore?

*Title from the song by Kate and Anna McGarrigle. Roughly translated it
means, 'We've been doing politics for a long time'*

I tell you, we can trust
in these irregular festivities.
See how the village treats us
with nougat, with flares and fireworks,
and such sighs sent after soaring rockets,
and how the heads tilt
till they hurt
to see the smoke rush over,
in the stinging sweet
cordite
night


## Café des Colonnes, Riberac

The waiter in his black waistcoat
running and running
through the jardin des Anglais
Market day with Karrimors and lollipops
'Will you look after Maisie?'
Push and pull
The weather forecast
orageux in le Sud-Ouest
and the rain
the rain
on red umbrellas
petunias tattering
puddles
in Ricard ashtrays
wet Gauloises
wet sugar
scalding breath of wet Alsatians

## Sunday in February

An apple bitten once
and spat in the gutter
glows bright
*it is past, it is wasted*

The corpse must go fully dressed
into the fire
with its Sunday shoes shining
*it is past, it is wasted*

Work, meetings, motherhood,
the discipline of hours and service
stretch thin in the running rain
oh, it could all snap
like a black bootlace

I could die on Sundays
and lie clotted and cold

*while the rain washes
the ashes of my father
down the slate sides of the mountains*

## Pushing forty

Just before winter
we see the trees show
their true colours:
the mad yellow of chestnuts
two maples like blood sisters
the orange beech
braver than lipstick

Pushing forty, we vow
that when the time comes
rather than wither
ladylike and white
we will henna our hair
like Colette, we too
will be gold and red
and go out
in a last wild blaze

# Women in the Cold War

Outside, time and famous dates passed –
Korea Suez Cuba Algeria all cannoned by
casually as a slap on the back.
In the butcher's and the grocer's,
not a word of them. No, only talk of
the sun, snow, seasons;
stillbirths, new banns posted;
the harvest, the Gala,
the Foot and Mouth which closed farm roads,
the Compensation.
As for violence, we had our own –
a thousand cattle burned in pits
a labourer, demented, raped a child
fine swimmers drowned in the loch's depths.
And most Saturdays some girl's wedding
brought the women clattering
down the High Street – they'd bang
on doors along the way and put up the cry,
then hang back respectfully and squint
at the hired cars, the ceremonial clothes.
My mother, her mother's mother
were brides like these,
country brides teetering up
the gravel-chipped path to the Kirk,
shielding their new shoes from scrapes.
By the sandstone wall, photos were posed,
against a bleak swell of lowland hills;
the photos show puckered faces
and a wind which whips the stiff bouquets.
The dances came and went, and fashions;
my girlfriends and I – in tight skirts
(or tiered), beads which popped
and hooped net petticoats –

crushed into cars and choked
on our own close scent, and smoke, and compliments.
But soon they sobered and they planned –
knitted cardigans all summer, by January
scanned the catalogues for cottons,
drab (for work), dressy (for holidays).
I saw them smooth
and full-blown dreaming of marriage
when I was still pockmarked with envy
and a thousand wants. I became crazy:
'I'll be an artist' I said ·
and bristled for the skirmish; quite slowly
their eyes scaled and their good sense
bunched against me.
'That's no' for the likes o' us.'
Elizabeth, Elaine, Rhoda of the long legs,
all matrons, mothering, hurrying
their men to work at 7am.
Now hunched round prams,
what landmarks of content do they stake out
as the village circles?
As tractors streak the fields with lime
and all the old women, hushed,
move to the funeral to see the flowers.

## August 6, 1945

In the Enola Gay
five minutes before impact
he whistles a dry tune

Later he will say
that the whole blooming sky
went up like an apricot ice.
Later he will laugh and tremble
at such a surrender, for the eye
of his belly saw Marilyn's skirts
fly over her head for ever

On the river bank,
bees drizzle over
hot white rhododendrons

Later she will walk
the dust, a scarlet girl
with her whole stripped skin
at her heel, stuck like an old
shoe sole or mermaid's tail

Later she will lie down
in the flecked black ash
where the people are become
as lizards or salamanders
and, blinded, she will complain:
Mother you are late, so late

Later in dreams he will look
down shrieking and see

ladybirds
ladybirds

*Enola Gay was the name of the plane which dropped the Hiroshima bomb*

# The edge of the ice

Maybe on a day like this:
hoar-frost in the park,
Sunday strollers
smothering the ice
with bread enough for the whole winter,
and the geese skidding,
with their wingbeat thunder
juddering the edges
and the trapped amoebic
blue bubbles – round,
perfect as planets –
their reverberation tearing the frill
of still papers
and the factory colours
and the words frozen but still shouting

Maybe on a day like this
on this perfect planet
we will see rainbow streaks
before the stretched blue
bubble of sky
bursts and empties
and hear at the edge of the ice
the future creak and enter

# East is East, and West is West

*(after a TV panel discussion about the New Physics)*

The physicist has fine hands
and is humble, remembering
Everest with her elvish winds
and the echo of the blue chambers
of ice

He is telling us we *are*
the elm, and the silted grass
after the monsoon, the rat, the dragonfly
and the high thistle, and the crows
climbing the steps of the trees,
branch to branch,
hopping and flapping

He is saying simply we know
when we are spoiling the earth,
that hurt mother on whose
arms we twirl and twirl
(and his hands flaunting boundaries,
opening hearts, inviting us in)

Intuitive awareness cuts no ice
with the man with the face
like a filing cabinet.
'Surely it can't be said that this is science?'
His mouth is a halfway grin
but oh how his hands refuse. If
he cannot finger it to ribbons
it is bad, bad, he will spit it out,
he will drum his heels on his steel chair

It is no business of his to believe,
or wonder with what dance we
will now placate the dead animals

He is back in the glue of the womb
He is fighting for mastery
and partitions

## Butterfingers

At last I have heard
that yell my mother
staunched, for there she was,
a presence of a kind,
aproned, broad back
baking grudges;
she stuck it out, me
the mouse at her heel,
the trailing tail, skinny
squeak which wavered through
decades now thunders up

Mother you filled my mouth with flour
lover you splashed your white
in the bowl of me
these hands slippery from not
holding have let me crash,
such noise and crackle
such mess to mop

But at the yolk I run
yellow,
yellow and good.

## City lights I

I had been weeping and spitting out
the sick talk of snakes
and death;
the night was foul yellow
and the fog whispered of
river bridges.
Each man who winked
had a killing in his eye.
Come on then, come and get me,
I'm weary of putting my fists up.
I could be shameless, loose
my skin and let it drop,
to welcome in the velvet
armies of the night.
For how deep the dark goes in
and all the lights melt into one
and all the lights melt into one

# City lights II

*Christmas*


Space race:
Oxford Street was eyes of glass,
astronauts, a Sugar-Plum fairy,
a window blinking with televisions.

Red laser beams pierce the street:
sight fails in splinters
before the sparkling jig of atoms,
the creation of Coherent Light
targetting past the horizon.
Eyes and hearts have limits
that have been reached.

The televisions flicker and fix:
the Earth is a blue balloon,
men dance the muffled
dance of toys on the dry rock
and suck at the dust of the moon
and suck at the dust of the moon

*Coherent Light is the scientific name given to the light which composes laser
beams*

# Heart of April

Upside down
in a magnolia tree
I dangle
in a sea of heaped sky
a soup
brimming with white flowers.

The sky is full of fevers,
greenbronze,
colour of dragons,
and in the city streets
the sour thunder dust
as the air
bears low.

Dissatisfaction sounds
like an axe
cracking sticks.
I am narrowed down to bones
shin bones across his legs
bones sticking in his teeth.

I will not be a midden-hen,
thin and grubbing.
I am winged and webbed
I am bigger than this.
Bright, formless, fluctuating.

## The Hallowe'en witch

*(for the wire-cutters at Greenham Common, 31 October 1983)*

She who slips out
of doors in the hour
between blindness
and enchantment
must be flotsam or
trouble

After the moon goes down
and the cameras are asleep
she does butterfly-balance
on the turn of the night
where the weathers set sail

Safer than shuttered houses
in the space she waits
while soldiers in their muttering beds
suckle like cats at the blankets
and dream of a long eye entering,
the wall open wide

Only in the morning
she is busy and small and
they will not know her
as she wipes the scattered
sun like dust from her
black clothes
and hides in the city's
grinding eye

## kisses for Mayakovsky

lacy rain
on the window
out there

lazybones
feet up
mooning in the smoke

percolator
spits in the kitchen

the sky
out there
bubbles up with planes

Mayakovsky said
'One must tear happiness
from the days to come'

gasometers bristle
like bad dreams
out there

let us hop like fleas across the lawn